Financial Freedom Formula

The Fastest Way To Real Estate Wealth

Augie Byllott
2nd Edition

CLAIM YOUR FREE GIFT FROM AUGIE!

WWW. CREATING WEALTH BLUEPRINT .COM

Table of Contents

Legal Disclaimers and Notices.........................4

Introduction..6

Chapter One..12

    This is Your Time

Chapter Two..18

    Transaction Engineering 101

Chapter Three..23

    My Favorite Technique

Chapter Four...28

    Creating & Presenting Offers

Chapter Five...34

    Deal Structure

Chapter Six...40

    Actual Case Study

Chapter Seven...45

    What's Next?

Legal Disclaimers and Notices

This eBook is presented to you for informational purposes only and is not a substitution for any professional advice. The contents herein are based on the views and opinions of the author and all associated contributors.

While every effort has been made by the author and all associated contributors to present accurate and up to date information within this document, it is apparent technologies rapidly change. Therefore, the author and all associated contributors reserve the right to update the contents and information provided herein as these changes progress. The author and/or all associated contributors take no responsibility for any errors or omissions if such discrepancies exist within this document.

The author and all other contributors accept no responsibility for any consequential actions taken, whether monetary, legal, or otherwise, by any and all readers of the materials provided. It is the reader's sole responsibility to seek professional advice before taking any action on their part.

Reader's results will vary based on their skill level and individual perception of the contents herein, and thus no guarantees, monetarily or otherwise, can be made accurately. Therefore, no guarantees are made.

Introduction & WEALTH System™

For over 18 years I have been coaching and mentoring friends and students in the transformation from a life working for *the man*…to a life of personal flexibility, high value contribution, wealth creation and financial freedom.

The vehicle chosen here to establish such a life is rooted in the tried and true age old industry of Real Estate.

Why Real Estate? After all, there are several other asset classes that offer the proposition of riches and wealth.

For me there are a lot of reasons why Real Estate is the winning choice...but here are a few of my favorites:

- Real Estate is, well, *real*. You can see it, touch it, stand on it, sit on it, park on it, sleep on it…you get my point.

- You can get started in your own business without significant cash outlays.

- Tax advantages. Real Estate offers some of the best tax incentives and advantages of all asset classes.

- Everyone always needs a place to live and do business, so the industry is not going anywhere.

- There is an inherent community aspect to the Real Estate business you don't get with, say, the stock market.

- And the most important reason of all: *Leverage.* As you'll learn, real estate offers what I think are the greatest financial leverage points the business world has to offer.

In the 18 years I've been coaching and mentoring others and also the years prior that I spent building my own business and its systems - I have learned, practiced, developed and refined strategies and systems that are proven winners for both new and experienced real estate investors.

In doing so I have developed a 6 Step WEALTH SYSTEM ™ that is the foundation of everything that we do in Real Estate Investing.

W.E.A.L.T.H

SYSTEM™

BUILD YOUR REAL ESTATE EMPIRE WITHOUT BANKS, CASH OR CREDIT

Step 1: W – Where are the Deals?

Step 2: E – Evaluate Motivation

Step 3: A – Analyze the What's & Why's

Step 4: L – Lay Out the Plan

Step 5: H – Have Your Exits

I'm excited for the first time here to share this process with you in this book.

This business has created a life for me (and countless others) that is free of the 9 to 5, or should we say now, the 7 to 7 grind that makes other business owners rich. And, instead, I have replaced that with a way to feed my family, grow my business and expand my wealth base as I go along.

But it wasn't always that way for me. I wasn't born with a silver spoon in my mouth by any stretch.

I was born in the Bronx , New York to a large family and raised on Long Island. The eldest of 6 kids, I not only had to fend for myself, I was fending for others also, and at a very early age.

I learned a lot about entrepreneurship by running the proverbial paper route. I ran the paper route because it was the only way I could make money to be able to afford the little extras for myself.

I like to laugh about the fact that I learned my early negotiating skills in middle school while sitting in the middle of my Italian friends and my Irish friends who argued and bickered with each other all the time. Being half of each nationality, I was always mediating between the two.

Making my way through school, and subsequently surviving various entrepreneurships as a bar owner and poker player, I ended up in a what many would consider a respectable corporate job, as an executive for Citibank.

It was there that I came to a stark realization. I did not own my own life. I was committed to the wealth creation of a corporate giant. That commitment required many hours of my life each week. As an executive, that commitment followed me home, nights and weekends.

Once I exhausted all these weekly hours, I was left with a meager number of hours to spend with my family and then the afterthought, what about my financial future?

Listen, I'm not complaining, nor am I knocking the millions of respected individuals who work hard in this lifetime to earn an education and live this American dream. I have nothing but the utmost respect for each and every one of you.

I'm just saying, it's not too long before this dream of ours can turn into struggles dealing with a lack of time, a lack of upward mobility, a lack of a financial foundation for our future, and a lack of freedom for the life we're leading now…while we're still young, healthy and vibrant!

If you can relate to any of this you're not alone. If you're ready to start the next chapter in your life, one that puts you on the path of freedom…freedom of time, financial freedom, and contribution to your family and community - then you are in the right place.

Welcome to our family. A community of likeminded individuals who support each other in this endeavor.

Please read on as I introduce you to the world of *Financial Freedom Formula - The Fastest Way To Real Estate Wealth.*

Augie Byllott

Chapter 1

This Is Your Time

"Success is what happens when preparation and action meet opportunity."

Augie Byllott

There are plenty of great deals out there and **they keep getting better**. Just remember to be a reluctant buyer, not a motivated buyer.

Take Your Time

Be selective and know your exit strategy.

In this market, my favorite strategy for building wealth is to buy and hold because when the next round of inflation hits, paper money won't keep its value but hard assets (like gold, houses, even securities) will rise.

Additionally, when we buy right, we can also accumulate properties that cash flow and produce current income.

It's Not All Bad News

Even during the worst housing crisis in recent memory, there were millions of homes in America that did not go into default and do you know why? Just like today, many are owned free and clear.
That's Right, They Have No Mortgage

When these properties sell, they allow the seller to become your financier. Even when banks don't lend, sellers do! Seller financing has to be my favorite form of financing because sellers have only one goal and that is to sell their property.

Banks look at the property as collateral; they don't care what property you buy.

But The Seller Truly Has a Vested Interest

That means that in order to sell quickly or to get their price, they are frequently willing to be flexible on terms. And that, is really good news!

You can negotiate a better deal with a property owner than you can with a bank because banks are basically large, inflexible, heavily regulated institutions that cannot act quickly. They aren't known for their creativity or flexibility either.

Sellers Can Be More Flexible

When dealing directly with a property owner we can negotiate many elements of the financing including: interest rate, term, payment amount and even when the payments will begin. Sometimes we can even get them to provide us repair money.

Think About It...

A $100,000 house that needs $10,000 in repairs and you could effectively borrow all of the money from the seller and pay them in monthly installments (then you as the investor might only have to come up with $10,000 because the rest is in the equity of the house).

You complete the repairs, get a tenant and then begin making the payments. Could you ever do that with a bank?

Granted This Is An Extreme Example

But a motivated seller may be happy to have his problem solved.

We once had a seller willing to give us $18,000 cash and a Mercedes SUV to solve his problem. Now that's motivation!

You Can Negotiate To Make The Mortgage Assumable

Something more common in today's market would be to negotiate seller financing without a due-on-sale clause which could then make the mortgage assumable.

This effectively allows you to re-sell the property with owner financing, on lease option, or with a wrap-around mortgage.

Real Estate Entrepreneurs Get Paid For Solving Problems

And, the more problems we solve for sellers and buyers alike, the more *profits we create*.

Real estate is a fairly illiquid asset and since the housing recovery and imposition of more stringent government regulations, many Americans are still experiencing serious obstacles to buying a home or investment property. Only a few loan products are available and qualifying for those that are available have become increasingly difficult

This is where savvy real estate entrepreneurs have an opportunity to build incredible fortunes...*by using their intellectual capital.*

Use Intellectual Capital or Brain Power!

The beauty of this market is that there are no limits because so many people need our help. By learning to buy and sell using creative financing techniques, you will serve a great many people and leave your competition in the dust.

In the following pages we'll discuss my favorite financing technique. The best part is that *anyone can learn to do this.*

Chapter 2

Transaction Engineering 101

"In order to succeed, we must first believe that we can. "

Michael Korda

This model works in all markets, anywhere in the country, but it works best in markets that lack liquidity (that is, available bank financing).

It works with residential as well as commercial real estate. And the technique is simple to use and only requires common sense and a little understanding of numbers.

I Know You Don't Like Math!

As my friend Gary Johnston likes to say, "it's not math...it's money." And he's right. Here's the good news. You can easily build an entire business around this model because each step in the buying and selling process can be made easy and systematic. I've been using it as part of my business for years.

Here's The Model:

First, Become a Transaction Engineer

Think of all the ways we could engineer or structure a transaction to buy property as a 'transaction engineer.'

To begin, we have four primary types of property you might target; they include:

- pretty houses,
- ugly houses,
- multi-family, or
- commercial property

Next, Use "No Bank" Acquisition Strategies

There are a variety of NO BANK NEEDED acquisition strategies to buy or control the property; which include:

- options

- leases
- subject to
- owner financing
- paying all cash

Finally, Consider Your Exit Strategy

We have our exit strategies which help us get to the cash or cash flow. We can employ numerous ways to rent, sell or hold a property; such as:

- quick turning (a/k/a flipping)
- renting
- lease optioning
- retailing
- selling with owner financing

A good system addresses the whole transaction, from acquisition to disposition, and that's what differentiates the newbie from the seasoned pro.

Your Property Acquisition Method Determines Your Exit

Your property acquisition method will have more

influence on your exit strategy than virtually any other factor.

Transactions engineered with excellent terms at acquisition provide us the best alternatives in terms of exit strategy.

The secret that most successful investors know is that having multiple exit strategies for each property acquired lowers your risk and increases your income.

It's All About the Financing...

While it may sound counter-intuitive, profiting in real estate is as much about the financing as it is about the real estate.

You need to consider the quality and utility of what you buy, how you will finance it, and whether you will sell or rent it in order to maximize your profits.

This disciplined approach gives you a solid business model.

We all know there are multiple strategies to do great deals.

My Mastermind Students and I have made millions of dollars using all of them.

But There Is One Technique That Is My # 1 Favorite

You'll find out all about it in the next chapter.

Chapter 3

My Favorite Technique

"My main focus is on my game."
Tiger Woods

See The Ball, Be The Ball

If you remember the classic movie Caddy Shack, the wild and crazy Chevy Chase gave the young caddy, Donnie, a putting lesson and used a line echoed by golfers ever since. He instructed Donnie to, "See the ball, be the ball."

Well, I am a benefits-driven investor and whether it's wholesaling, retailing, lease options, rehabbing, short sales, or whatever, I look for the technique which provides the most benefits for each transaction.

See the Bank, Be The Bank

But, my favorite technique provides the maximum benefit while eliminating virtually all the transaction related hurdles real estate entrepreneurs face. It is a truly powerful technique. I call this awesome technique, "Be the Bank."

Like Chevy Chase's, "See the ball, be the ball," I prefer, "See the Bank, Be the Bank."

No one Should restrict Your Ability To Do Business

As an entrepreneur, I don't want anyone or anything to restrict my ability to do business. Just look happened in the US economy...the banks couldn't perform so the country couldn't perform. That's absurd! This nation was built by people with ingenuity, energy and perseverance.

Focus On the Money Source

One of the major factors behind all success is focus. Isn't that the underlying message Chevy was giving young Donnie? Not just focus on our goal but focus on our process. The focus was on the ball rather than the cup.

In our case it is focus on the "Bank" or the money source. Without a process that assures proper focus we end up with unpredictable results. The more consistent our process, the more predictable our results.

This is How "Be the Bank" Works...

Begin by focusing on free and clear properties.

Seasoned real estate entrepreneurs know that when there's more equity in a deal, we have more ways to create offers and more exits. (No equity means you have fewer options because you will have to create equity by discounting the debt or waiting for the property to appreciate.)

More Equity = More Options

Benefits Of Focusing On Free And Clear Properties:

- ***The ability to buy using installments***; that is, paying the seller with a fixed monthly payment provided by the income from the property. This is because frequently sellers with free and clear properties do not need all of their equity in cash now. If they did, they could easily have pulled it out sooner.

- *The flexibility to borrow against the equity* (without using a bank) by using hard money, private investors or better yet – the seller. This can provide funds for buying, holding and getting a house occupied with little or no out- of-pocket expenses.

- *The possibility of negotiating very favorable financing terms.* The seller's goal is to sell the property so they may be willing to offer low or no interest, deferred payments, additional repair funds, etc.

- *By having them finance the sale, you can help them defer or reduce their tax bill.* Many free and clear properties are non-owner occupied and the seller could face a big tax bill if they collected all their cash at once.

- *You might find landlords with multiple properties* who want to eliminate all their management hassles and sell their portfolio. They may even be willing to start by leasing the properties to you with options to buy (so you can generate cash flow) and then buy them on a tax efficient schedule.

- *You can even re-sell the property* and offer seller financing to your buyer by leveraging the existing financing you just created with the seller.

Chapter 4
Creating and Presenting Offers

Our imagination is the only limit to what we can hope to have in the future."

Charles F. Kettering

Terms Are The Key

Now we create offers based on the monthly payment and end up with low or 0% seller financing.

Long term seller financing reduces my resistance to price because it really doesn't matter what price a seller wants with a free and clear property. I can always pay it. Terms are the key.

I frequently ask my seminar attendees if anyone is willing to sell me their house for a million dollars. Lots of hands go up and then I tell them they'll receive $1.00 a month for one million months! So when it comes to price, the only question is, "how long do I have to pay?" The longer they can wait, the more I can pay.

OH the Benefits!!

Here Are The Benefits Of Creating A Seller-Held
Note At Low Or 0% Interest:

- *Low or close-to-0% interest allows us to offer a higher purchase price* and get more of our offers accepted by having the seller defer payment on part or all of their equity.

- *You could offer a balloon payment* due in several years and enjoy the cash flow from the property until the balloon comes due. Personally, I think this choice is a little short sighted. History has taught me that balloon payments always come due at the most inconvenient time. However, you can protect yourself with a simple clause in the note which allows for an extension until borrowing rates improve.

- *Build a large equity position* by giving all the positive cash flow (cash above taxes, insurance and maintenance) to the seller and quickly pay down the principle. Again, not your best choice.

- *Low Monthly Payments Maximize Cash Flow...Structure the payments low enough that the property will cash flow from day one.* Rents will rise over time and so will your net cash flow. Over 10 to 20 years the value of the property will rise and so will rents. Now you're creating wealth with a low fixed payment. A very good choice!

But Wait, There's More!

More Benefits!!

- *You can increase your yield by offering multiple payments in exchange for a discount*; i.e., "Mr. Seller, if you ever need a lump of cash, I'll give 3 payments in advance for a 10% discount or 6 payments for a 15% discount." That's like getting one or two months free. The seller gets a nice lump of cash and you get a great yield. An even better choice!

- *You can discount the entire note at an even larger yield* if the seller wants to be paid off early. That's the deal after the deal...extra profit!

• Lastly, when **negotiating seller held financing, we can** *negotiate the ability to substitute collateral* (move the mortgage to another property) *or subordinate the mortgage* so that you can borrow on the property and the seller note remains in second position.

That's financial flexibility!

That is a whole lot of benefit, I think you'll agree.

Create Predictable Profit On Every Deal...

Your Seller Will Often Take a 10 to 20% Discount if you do this...

You may get a seller to take a 10 to 20% discount by using the cost-to-sell guidelines. Show the seller what he might net by selling his or her house traditionally.

This is done by subtracting all selling expenses (real estate commission, closing costs, holding costs, maintenance and home inspection, "gotcha's," etc.) from their asking price.

Ask If You Can Make A Small Profit...Yeah, Really!

Sometimes you can get them to go even a little lower by asking if it's okay if you make a small profit on the deal. Then lower again if you take the property 'as is.' And even lower if you give them some or all of their equity in cash now instead of later.

Buy At A Discount, Sell At a Premium

If you can reasonably estimate the price, you can sell the house by offering owner financing or a lease option to your buyer. You can then calculate the maximum allowable price you can pay the seller.

If you can buy at a discount with seller financing, and keep that financing in place and sell at a premium, there should be little difficulty creating a 15 to 25% equity spread. But remember:

Holding for years rather than months is where you begin to build wealth.

Use Flexible Exits...

Rent or Sell with Owner Financing, or Lease Option ASAP!

Since the mortgage meltdown, liquidity crisis, and new government regulations, sellers are having trouble selling and buyers are having trouble buying unless they are prepared to pay **all cash**.

Virtually all loans for buyers with a marginal credit score are gone. Even good credit buyers in many cases are being left wanting. This lack of mortgage money has created a growing demand for rentals and the need for **creative seller financing**. This is and will likely remain the "Perfect Storm" for savvy investors for years to come.

This awesome technique is the solution... *BE THE BANK!*

Chapter 5

Deal Structure

"Our imagination is the only limit to what we can hope to have in the future."

Charles F. Kettering

Be the Bank...

When you've created 0% seller financing on a house you've bought, you're like a bank borrowing from the Fed! How quickly do you want to pay it off? Never! Then how can you sell?

You simply sell to a tenant buyer and insist they close with a wrap-around mortgage or similar owner financing instrument (just like a bank) after they complete their term in a lease option.

Or...Close Right Way With A 'Wrap'

Find a buyer with more money down and close now with 'wraparound owner financing' (just like a bank). Or, just rent it, and let your tenant buy the property for you.

Using a "Wrap Around Mortgage," "Contract for Deed" or "Agreement for Deed" (whichever is the standard in your part of the country), your buyer will make a monthly payment to you, and you make your payment on the underlying seller financing to your seller. *The difference is your monthly cash flow.*

This is How it Works...

Option #1:

Give Your Seller Some Cash Now And Some Cash Later.

Your seller has a pretty house worth $220,000 in today's market, it needs no repairs and is owned free and clear but the seller has difficulty finding a buyer and wants to sell now.

The market is slow and they need to sell now. You estimate that within 60 days you can find a buyer that will pay $220,000.

You will finance $200,000 at 6% or $1,000 a month interest-only payments with a $20,000 down payment.

What If The Seller Demands His Full Price?

It would be easy to show the seller that $200,000 is a fair price when taking into account 10% for normal sales costs.

But what if the seller demands his full price of $220,000 with $20,000 down? Could you actually pay that much? Yes, you can. You could give the seller $20,000 (from the end buyer) now and $200,000 as a lump sum balloon payment due in 7 years.

This way they get their price and some cash now with the balance coming later.

What Do You Get In Return?

From your buyer, you get $1,000 a month for 84 months or $84,000 with no property management!

At the end of 7 years you owe $200,000 to the seller but your buyer still owes you $200,000 (as the $1,000/month was interest-only payments; nothing was paid towards the principal).

You've earned $84,000 in 7 years!

In spite of the fact that you owe and are owed $200,000, you've earned $84,000 during those 7 years.

So now you see the power that comes when you choose to "Be the Bank"!

Option #2:

Give /The Seller The Cash Flow And You Get Cash At Both Ends.

You use the same scenario as above but the seller agrees to nothing down. Now you can pay the seller $1,000 principal-only payments each month instead.

In this case you keep the $20,000 from your buyer. In 7 years you owe the seller $136,000 (remember, you paid $1,000 per month for 84 months towards

the principle) but your buyer still owes you
$200,000.

That's A $64,000 Back-End Payday!

This gives you tremendous leverage, not to mention
the impact on your financial situation if you did 10
or 20 of these transactions. The cumulative effect
can be staggering.

Option 3

**You Give The
Seller Monthly
Payments And
Arbitrage The
Money**

**Arbitrage is
basically is
taking
advantage of
a price
difference.
"An arbitrage
is a purchase
of an asset in
one market for the purpose of making that
asset available in another market to take
advantage of inequities in price. In real**

estate, when you wholesale or flip a property you are in effect participating in a type of real estate arbitrage."

With everything being the same, you give the seller $20,000 down and 200 monthly payments of $1000 each. What you have here is an interest free loan, no balloon. Then, you finance your buyer at 6% amortizing or $1,199.10 per month for 360 months.

You've Created A Cash Machine...

Effectively you have just created a cash machine which will generate $200 per month cash flow for 200 months or $40,000.

Plus... the buyer will make an additional 160 payments of $1,199.10 each which means you make another $192,000! The total profit on this deal is $232,000 (assuming the loan goes the full 30 years).

It's A Beautiful Strategy

Even if your buyer sells in the future, your underlying loan is paying down at a much faster rate, thereby providing you an increasing equity position.

Chapter 6

Actual Case Study

"It's not math...it's money."

Gary Jonhston

Creating Your Own Early Retirement Plan...

CASE STUDY (for illustration purposes only):

One of my coaching clients will make over $400,000 on a single deal using this strategy:

She mailed out a few probate letters and found the owner of a free and clear house he inherited.

He complained about having to maintain the property and he really wanted to sell it now but the market was slow. The house was worth about $250,000 and needed only minor clean up. It had a good floor plan and sat on a small lake in a desirable residential community.

The House Was Free And Clear

Since the house was free and clear, she offered to buy the house for $200,000 and pay the owner $1,000 a month until paid (200 months or 16 1/2 years). Because it needed a little work and she needed time to find a tenant, payments would begin 90 days after closing.

You read that right, **she asked for the payments to begin 3 months after closing and he agreed.** Do you see what happens when you ask? You can negotiate anything! She actually had a tenant move in within 30 days of closing and 2 months before the first payment was due!

200 months X $1000 = $200,000 - $2000 (2 months rent)=
$198,000

Her plan is to rent the property at $1,300 a month for the next 10 years and then sell it with 40 year owner financing for about $350,000.

120 months (10 years) of payments at $1000 means she's paid $120,000 toward the $200,000 she owed leaving a balance on the mortgage of $80,000.

In that time, rents and values are likely to rise and by the end of the 10 years she will owe the original seller only $80,000 and have a house worth $350,000! She'll have created $270,000 in equity!

When she sells it for $350,000 with owner-financing, she'll collect over $2,500 a month but only pay out $1,000 a month to the original seller on the remaining balance of $80,000.

That's right; she will clear about **$18,000** a year for the next 7 years.

$2,500 a month (incoming) - $1,000 (outgoing) = $1,500

$1,500/month X 12 months = $18,000 a year

$18,000 a year X 7 years = **$126,000 total income**

Once the underlying mortgage is paid off, she will still collect $2,500 a month income with no outgoing payment. That's $30,000 income per year for the remaining 29 years.

What If The Buyer Sells Early?

Let's say her buyer sells the property and pays her off after only 80 months; the same amount time it will take to pay off the underlying mortgage.

Remember, that is the number number of payments left on the original $200,000 mortgage when she sold the property.

Her Earnings Would Look Something Like This:

Rent spread first 10 years
$ 15,250*
Payment spread next 80 months
$126,000
Remaining equity due
$322,563* *

Total
$463,813

*   *After taxes & insurance, assumes a 3% annual rent increase*
* * *Based on a 7.75% interest rate paid by the buyer*

Even more benefits...

A couple of other soft benefits include the fact that her profit will be taxed at the long term capital gains rate.

And her other income will be offset by the expenses and depreciation during the period she holds the property as a rental, and she now has an excellent income stream to supplement her retirement.

That's what I call maximizing her intellectual capital!

Chapter 7

What's Next?

*"If you don't know where
you're going, any road will get you there."*

Cheshire Cat, Alice In Wonderland

Where Do We Go From Here?

What's your plan for the future? Will you work until you are 65 or 70? The average retiree today at age 65 has less than $70,000 in assets and social security (for as long as it lasts). That is no way to end up after a lifetime of work. Maybe it is time to build your own personal economy. Real estate can provide the building blocks for creating that economy.

Are you tired of others setting your worth? When was the last time you got a raise that really reflected your true value? Who is in control of your life, your future?

At *Creating Wealth* we help investors put the pieces together using a simple easy to use 5 Step Real Estate Wealth System. What if you could buy properties in your market without using lots of cash or credit?

Imagine replacing your current income and working because you *choose* to rather than because you have to? What would it be like to wake up every morning and do something you truly love?

If you enjoyed the strategies and ideas presented in this book we would love to help you apply these and other great *Transaction Engineering* strategies and techniques while starting, building or growing your own real estate investment business.

If you are tired of trying things that don't work you can do one of three things:

1. **You can do nothing** - this will allow you to maintain the status quo until something beyond your control might change the course of your career or even the state of your employment.

2. **You can try it on your own** - I did and it took more over 10 years to gain real traction. Most folks that take this approach don't last 24 months.

3. **You can take effective action** shorten your learning curve, and massively increase your effectiveness.

No matter what your experience level, we offer our clients the opportunity to generate current income, build a tax advantaged real estate portfolio or bolster their retirement assets using real estate as the primary vehicle.

After all, isn't it about lifestyle? Are you looking for more family time? Freedom from financial worry? The ability to be well paid for work you can be proud of? And best of all, build a legacy for future generations.

When you have the right tools in your tool kit, both new and experienced investors can learn to recognize and maximize real estate investment opportunities in any market.

At **Creating Wealth** we work with our clients to eliminate stumbling blocks, increase their effectiveness and become more successful.

Here is what our students are saying:

Sergey and I achieved our goal of closing four deals this year. This past Friday, we closed deal #5 & deal #6 (yes, two deals in one day!). We are pretty happy about our results... and we still have two more months to go.

> **Dan Wall**
> **Full Time Real Estate Investor**

"Augie continues to impress me with his knowledge and understanding of investing in real estate. He has a sincere desire to share his wisdom and is a great mentor!

Augie's coaching and teaching style are absolutely second to none. As a full-time investor myself, I highly recommend his programs to any investor seeking to improve their investing skills and grow their wealth. Thanks Augie, for your consistent guidance and encouragement!"

Charles A. Fischer
Real Estate Investor and Coach

Last month, Augie Byllott challenged his new students and the alumni present at an event to do a creatively structured deal in the next month. My husband and I both accepted the challenge and as of today, we have achieved the goal with two new creative deals ready to close this month. Thank you to Augie and to Creating Wealth for equipping us with the knowledge and the confidence to create winning solutions for everyone involved!

Marlena Dates
Full Time Mom and Real Estate Investor

Real estate has created more millionaires than any other asset class and has been doing so for decades. It is the only area I know where the average man or woman can compete with big business and be on a level playing field.

At Creating Wealth we believe in safe profitable investing and our clients learn to do two things very well:

1. Play Full Out and,

2. Take Effective Action

The result is increased confidence, more income and the ability to create their own personal economy!

Thanks for reading my book and I wish you tremendous success!

You can contact us at
WeCare@CreatingWealthUSA.com

"You can have excuses or results... but not both!"
Augie Byllott

Augie Byllott is a husband, father, real estate investor, speaker and coach.

Through his real estate investment company Homeowner Resource, LLC, he specializes in all facets of residential real estate investing.

He is also a nationally recognized author, trainer, success coach and speaker who teaches creative real estate investing to people from all walks of life.

His inspiring and principle oriented approach to business has helped him earn a highly respected position in the wealth building and educational arena.

*Augie believes in creating win/win scenarios through **Transaction Engineering**. He is the Chief Entrepreneurial Officer of Creating Wealth USA, a company dedicated to providing education and training systems for real estate investors.*

***Creating Wealth** teaches methods for wealth creation through real estate investing, and provides training programs on two levels: one level for the informed investor, and another for the novice.*

*By promoting fair play and ethical practices, **Creating Wealth** teaches clients how to create win/win solutions for sellers, buyers and tenants.*

Many subject areas are covered, including;

- ***Wealth Building and Exit Strategies,***
- ***Exploding Your Retirement Account,***
- ***Due Diligence-What To Do Before You Buy,***
- ***Negotiating Skills Training,***
- ***Building Your Private Money Network,***

- *Creating Positive Leverage,*
- *Buying Houses Subject-To,*
- *Creating Wealth With Lease Options, and more...*

Augie has served on the Legislative Committees of both The Central Florida Realty Investor Association and The National Real Estate Investor Association. He is also a Lifetime and Advisory Board member of one of the nation's largest Real Estate Investor Associations in the nation.

*He writes numerous articles on the subject of creative real estate investing, financial literacy and living with abundance for investment associations and also through his newsletter called **The Intellectual Capital Report**.*

*If you'd like to sign up for our complimentary newsletter, or learn more about our coaching programs or live training events, please visit **www.CreatingWealthUSA.com**.*

Copyright © 2019 by Augie Byllott

All rights reserved.

No part of this book may be reproduced in any form or by any electronic or mechanical means including information storage and retrieval systems, without permission in writing from the author. The only exception is by a reviewer, who may quote short excerpts in a review.

Printed in the United States of America

2019

Made in the USA
Columbia, SC
23 September 2023

23099977R00030